MY QUICK WRITES

My Quick Writes

FOR INSIDE WRITING

Donald H. Graves
and
Penny Kittle

HEINEMANN
Portsmouth, NH

Heinemann

361 Hanover Street
Portsmouth, NH 03801–3912
www.heinemann.com

Offices and agents throughout the world

Library of Congress Cataloging-in-Publication Data
Graves, Donald H.
    My quick writes : for inside writing / Donald H. Graves and Penny Kittle.
       p. cm.
    ISBN 0–325–00838–8
    1. Authorship.   2. Creative writing.   I. Kittle, Penny.   II. Title.
PN145.G69 2005
808′.02—dc22

          2005012345

Editor: Lois Bridges
Developmental editor: Alan Huisman
Production editor: Abigail M. Heim
Typesetter: Technologies 'N Typography
Text and cover design: Joyce Weston Design
Manufacturing: Louise Richardson

Printed in the United States of America on acid-free paper
19   18   17   VP   13   14

CONTENTS

Introduction   1

Getting Started: The First 30 Quick Writes   6

Point of View   40

Poetry   52

Letters into Essays   68

Fiction   76

Quick Writes for Children   85

Final Reflection   105

INTRODUCTION

Welcome to *My Quick Writes*, in which you will explore the writing process by writing rapidly on suggested topics or those of your own choosing.

First, let me tell you about my background as a writer. (It's a miracle that I'm writing these words.) Thanks to one teacher in my sophomore year in high school, in 1945, I stayed in the writing game. I'd asked her what I needed to do to become a writer, and she said, "Write and rewrite." She didn't show me how to write, but she didn't laugh at my desire to do it. In retrospect, I find it quite amazing that she took me seriously. But that candle of ambition managed to flicker in the darkness for the next thirty years.

The darkness of writing began with nasty comments on my papers in freshman composition. Since I chose to be an English major, I received more comments and corrections during the remainder of my college years. For my senior thesis, I poured out my heart on conscientious objection while writing about Prince Andrew Bolkonsky in Tolstoy's *War and Peace*. My professor wrote one line of comment: "D+, please change your typewriter ribbon." Later, when I was working toward my doctorate, my dissertation adviser wrote a note saying that perhaps I ought to take an English course to learn how to write.

In 1973 I met Donald Murray, a professor of English at the University of New Hampshire and the winner of a Pulitzer Prize in journalism. He read my work and pointed out that while most of my writing was pure dissertationese, a few lines sounded like me. He led me out of the wilderness of trying to please audiences, helped me oust my self-inflicted censor, and showed me how to find my voice, the thing that made my writing me. I was fortunate to run into such a writing teacher.

Whatever your own writing history, I suspect you realize that you have things to say. You joke with colleagues, "I should write that down. I know it would be a best-seller." Or, you threaten to fire off an irate note to the local newspaper. The reason you don't is that you don't have the time or you aren't comfortable with yourself as a writer. But you do have a voice that yearns to be heard.

As a way to help you uncover topics and ideas worth writing about, I want you to embark on a series of *quick writes*—thirty short jump-right-in pieces on anything that strikes you related to suggested prompts (numbers 29 and 30 are blank, for you to fill in with topics that occur to you while you are responding to the others). I've also included some samples as models of the quick, easy writing these topics are meant to inspire. I know you will find your voice in the process. You may not find it in every piece you write, but here and there you will identify lines and words you like. And you'll say, "Now if I could write more stuff like that I'd be a pretty good writer."

Here's how to begin.

1. Read over the first twenty-eight "starters" and choose four or five that you think are easy places for you to begin writing.

2. Then, for each prompt you've selected:

HEAR MORE ABOUT DON'S WRITING JOURNEYS IN THE WRITER'S LIFE INTERVIEW.

- Write rapidly for ten minutes.

- Change nothing.

- Lower your standards. (I know, you've been working all your life to raise standards and now I'm asking you to lower them. The point of a first draft is to let everything in without judging the quality of the piece. A quick first draft draws on the peripheral; one line may trigger something different in the next line. Later, I'll show you how to enjoy rereading your work.)

- Let your own thinking guide you, not the prompt.

There's an essential difference between these quick writes and traditional writing prompts. Look at the quick write about recess on page 90. If this were a writing prompt on an assessment, every student would be expected to write about recess. Not so with quick writes. If a student writes in her first sentence, "I remember our teacher Miss Duke watching us at recess" and continues thinking and writing about that teacher, we celebrate the writer's having found a seed idea that holds her interest. It doesn't matter if the writer says nothing at all about recess. Quick writes nudge us to discover topics that matter, not to respond to a question that may have nothing to do with our experience. When writing quickly, our own thoughts can surprise us. Quick writes seek diversity, not conformity.

Here's an example using quick write number 3:

> Think about a photograph you feel a strong emotional connection to, one of: a family gathering, you and your grandfather, your first communion, you and your spouse, a day at the beach. Tell who is in the photo and why you treasure it.

I'm going to use the following photo, which appears on the cover of my book *How to Catch a Shark*.

Here are some of the possibilities I might write about, some of the directions I might take.

- *The Toilet* sign. That toilet had a seat with a bucket. The smell was enough to knock anyone dead. I might have used it twice in twelve years.

- My friend Bob. He was three years younger, but his .22 rifle killed the shark.

- The story of catching the shark.

- The shack in the background belonged to my Uncle Nelson. I could write about my uncle.

- My pride in catching the shark. I couldn't catch anything, but I could catch a shark.

I think I'll write for ten minutes about the toilet.

People ask me about the shark in the photo, but the second thing people ask me, "Now about that sign, 'The Toilet,' what's that doing there?"

I usually ignore the question but not now. Open that door, my friends, and the stench will stop you in your tracks. This isn't a flush toilet. This is just a frame over a bucket.

As a kid I avoided that toilet like the plague. I'd walk a quarter of a mile back to the house to use the toilet at home before I'd walk in there. I'd see customers walk in there and come out with their heads shaking. They'd look at me and say, "How do you stand it?" or, "When are you going to dump that thing?"

I realize now that it was my Uncle Nelson who would take the bucket, scull a quarter of a mile out to sea, and then dump it. Indeed, until now it never occurred to me who dumped the bucket. Of course, Uncle Nelson would chuckle about the customers he'd lose for his boat business just because of that bucket. "Anybody who can stand the stink of bait ought to be able to take a piss in there." I guess he was right. ✎

Get the idea?

Now it's your turn to begin telling the stories of your life. I want you to do at least two ten-minute quick writes every day for two weeks. It may take several days to get used to following the guidelines. But by the ninth or tenth piece you'll find your stride. Turn the page and begin your own writing journey. Be playful with words. See what surfaces. Bon voyage!

GETTING STARTED: THE FIRST 30 QUICK WRITES

1. "When I was a kid I had certain chores I had to do. The first one was . . .". Write about that chore in all the detail you can remember and show your feelings about doing it.

_____

_____

_____

_____

_____

_____

_____

_____

_____

_____

_____

_____

_____

_____

_____

_____

_____

_____

_____

_____

_____

_____

2. Choose a scene featuring you and your favorite pet. "One time I was with my dog [my cat, my horse] and . . ."

_____

_____

_____

_____

_____

_____

_____

_____

_____

_____

_____

_____

_____

_____

_____

_____

_____

_____

_____

_____

_____

_____

_____

_____

3. Think about a photograph you feel a strong emotional connection to, one of: a family gathering, you and your grandfather, your first communion, you and your spouse, a day at the beach. Tell who is in the photo and why you treasure it.

_____

_____

_____

_____

_____

_____

_____

_____

_____

_____

_____

_____

_____

_____

_____

_____

_____

_____

_____

_____

_____

_____

4. Make a partial grocery list of what you need to buy for the weekend. Write about a food that gives you energy or that just plain tastes good.

5. Finish the phrase "I'm from . . ." with concrete images from your past. If you get stuck just write "I'm from" and finish the sentence with whatever pops into your head. (This pattern is inspired by a poem by George Ella Lyon. Penny's quick write for this prompt is on the next pages.)

Where I'm From

Penny Kittle

I'm from Belmont Street in Portland
just an alley away
from tall evergreens and vine raspberries in Mt. Tabor Park.
I'm from skinned knees and stubbed toes,
shooting hoops until the streetlight came on above the backboard
to call us home.
I'm from the pussywillow tree that draped long, spindly branches over the
   greenhouse roof creating a fort for me in the shelter of green.

I'm from "Time for dinner!" and "What can I get you to eat?"
lump-free mashed potatoes and gravy
roast beef and whole turkeys
bloated brussels sprouts and waxy limas I hid in my napkin
because the dog wouldn't eat 'em.
I'm from sugar cookies with elaborate icing
and cakes with multi-tiered roses.
I'm from homemade jams and donuts boiling in oil
then shook in a brown paper bag a quarter-full of cinnamon sugar
when friends spent the night.

I'm from a double bed I shared with my sister
whispering secrets across the covers
giggling in unison
until she went to high school.
I'm from Elton John records on a plastic orange record player
I'm from the Beach Boys
the Jackson Five
the Beatles
and always Elton
until I grew tougher and taller and discovered heavy metal.

I'm from an abandoned black cat we named Mickey Finn
stretching and purring on my head while I slept.
I'm from Holly the Christmas calico
and Butchie our scruffy mutt
who caught whole rocks between his teeth
and was dead to cancer before any of us were ready.

I'm from casting beside Dad on small, quiet streams
or near the roar of Bonneville Dam
steelhead and sturgeon and shad we caught in the ocean's surf.
I'm from grandpa's wood shop of toys and puzzles and bird mansions
dusty shelves and triangle mounds of sawdust
large hands holding tools in the light from tiny windows
teaching me.

I'm from teaching
and tennis
and my silver Mini Cooper.
I'm from twenty years of marriage to a man I still adore
and children so marvelous and funny I can't believe they're mine.
I'm from reading and writing and reading some more
with a large mug of coffee in one hand
and my favorite cartridge pen in the other.
I'm from the mountains of Oregon and the green of Washington state,
endless beaches in California
the hills near Cincinnati
the windy, cold winters of Michigan
to the wildlife in the mountains of New Hampshire.

I'm from here.
Now.
Teaching writing.

6. Once when I was learning how to drive I got going a little too fast, came around a curve, and was suddenly faced by a delivery truck coming straight at me. I overcompensated and whipped my wheel to the right and ended up in a swamp. Write about an incident when you were learning to drive. (Penny's response is on the next page.)

I'm behind the wheel of my grandfather's station wagon on a narrow, curvy road in southeast Portland with my father seated beside me reading the paper. I'm taking the corner too fast, hugging the edge of the road praying there won't be any walkers out so early this morning, and clenching my gut whenever a car comes towards me. I feel too close to cars and the embankment with no room between. My father whistles as he reads. I'm barely 15, out learning how to drive with Dad, but I'm learning at 35 mph on a stretch of road that has always made me nervous as a passenger, feeling tightly squeezed in a narrow canyon. My hands are shaking. My father keeps reading. Grandpa's slate blue station wagon goes as fast as I dare and I nudge the gas pedal harder as I notice my rearview mirror clogged with impatient drivers behind me. I know exactly how long this road is, how much farther I have to remain calm. I could turn off to the right, I see the escape approaching, but I keep the nose pointed forward and endure. No giving up. Dad turns the pages of the paper without a glance through the windshield to see if I'm even centered between the lines. Is this confidence or his own terror? I want help and I don't know how to ask.

7. Write about what you were doing at 5:00 PM yesterday.

8. I have a recurring dream where I ask in disbelief: "You mean *today* is the day of the test?" Write about taking a test.

9. Try writing in the voice of someone you know well. How does this person see the world? What is she or he thinking? Write in first person and present tense.

10. What stories do your hands tell? Trace around your hand and fill it in with memories that are connected to your hands. (Penny's response is on the next page.)

Here's Penny's response to quick write 10:

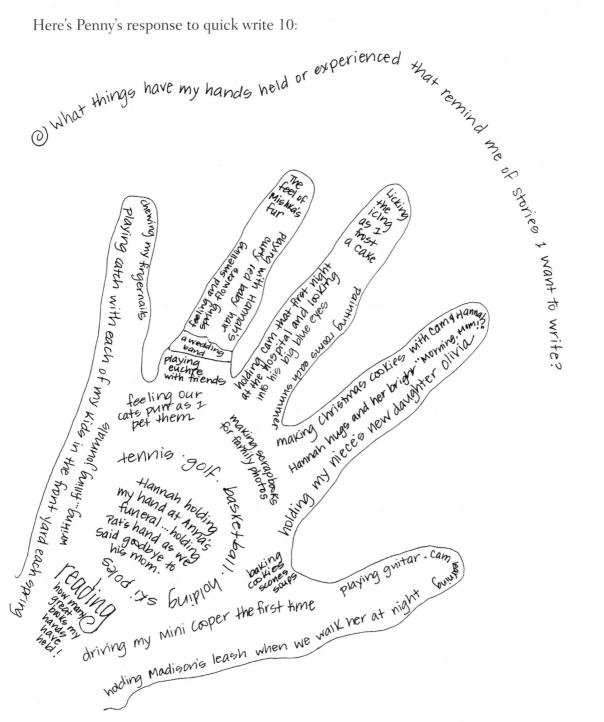

© What things have my hands held or experienced that remind me of stories I want to write?

The feel of Mishka's fur

Licking the icing as I frost a cake

feeling and smelling spring flowers

pushing red hair from Hannah's hair

painting rooms each summer

holding Cam that first night at the hospital and looking into his big blue eyes

a wedding band

playing euchre with friends

feeling our cats purr as I pet them

making scrapbooks for family photos

making Christmas cookies with Cam & Hannah

Hannah hugs and her bright "Morning, Mom!?"

holding my niece's new daughter Olivia

chewing my fingernails

playing catch with each of my kids in the front yard each spring ... filling journals

tennis . golf . basketball . holding ski poles

Hannah holding my hand at Anna's funeral ... holding Pat's hand as we said goodbye to his mom.

reading how many great books my hands have held!

baking cookies scones soups

playing guitar . Cam learning

driving my Mini Cooper the first time

holding Madison's leash when we walk her at night

11. What is there not enough of in your life right now, this very minute? Write about it.

12. Whom do you envy? What does this person have that you want? Write about this person.

13. Think back to when you had a confrontation with someone and walked away wishing you had said what you were thinking. Say it now. Write these thoughts, speaking directly to the person.

14. What gives you energy? What takes it away? What do you find a waste of time? Write the details that answer these three questions.

15. Think about a dance you went to in middle or high school. Zoom in on all the details you remember.

16. List the names of four students you feel strongly about. Choose one student and write why you feel strongly about him or her. (Watch Penny write about one of her students and discuss it with Don on the DVD in the **Conferring** section.)

17. Choose a new teacher in your school and write from that person's
point of view about what it's like to teach at your school.

18. Remember when school was canceled unexpectedly for a snowstorm, a power failure, or a flu epidemic? Were you a teacher or a student? How did you feel about it? Write as many details as you can.

19. Choose an important time in your life and list the music you remember connected to those memories. Write about that kind of music generally, or choose one particular song.

_____

_____

_____

_____

_____

_____

_____

_____

_____

_____

_____

_____

_____

_____

_____

_____

_____

_____

_____

_____

_____

_____

_____

_____

20. The phone rings; it's your mother. Write the dialogue of your conversation. Then write the dialogue of a phone conversation with your father. Write another piece discussing how these conversations are similar and how they are different.

_____

_____

_____

_____

_____

_____

_____

_____

_____

_____

_____

_____

_____

_____

_____

_____

_____

_____

_____

_____

_____

_____

_____

_____

_____

_____

21. Retell a family story you have heard told many times. Write your version of that story.

_____

_____

_____

_____

_____

_____

_____

_____

_____

_____

_____

_____

_____

_____

_____

_____

_____

_____

_____

_____

_____

_____

_____

22. How did your great grandfather die? Write that story if you know. Imagine it if you don't know. Or, write about how you could find out.

23. Think of someone who doesn't respect you or value what you offer. Write a letter that informs this person of your abilities as well as what the person needs to do to become acquainted with your abilities.

24. List three books that are important to you. Choose one and write about how it has affected your life.

25. If you have a niece, a nephew, a daughter, or a son, write about a special time you shared and the impression it made on you.

_____
_____
_____
_____
_____
_____
_____
_____
_____
_____
_____
_____
_____
_____
_____
_____
_____
_____
_____
_____
_____
_____
_____
_____
_____
_____
_____

26. Choose a certain food or dish that you enjoy eating. Tell about a time when you ate it. What about the taste do you especially enjoy?

27. People, especially in America, battle gaining weight. Write about your special battle (or nonbattle).

28. When someone says "My plate is already too full," what does that mean to you? Have you felt that way? What's on your plate? Imagine all the things you are carrying in your head and trying to manage each day, in both your teaching life and your personal life. Unload your mind; write it down.

_____

_____

_____

_____

_____

_____

_____

_____

_____

_____

_____

_____

_____

_____

_____

_____

_____

_____

_____

_____

29. Your choice. While writing previous quick writes, other topics probably occurred to you. Jot down one of them here and then write about it.

30. Your choice. While writing previous quick writes, other topics probably
occurred to you. Jot down one of them here and then write about it.

POINT OF VIEW

For purposes of the following quick writes, you'll be writing in the first person, present tense, about the same event as seen or experienced from different people's point of view. For example, here's an event:

> Mr. Wood's bus is the slowest bus to load. He's such a friendly man; he greets each child by name and chats with each one.

Write this scene from two or more of the following points of view: a child boarding the bus, the bus monitor, or Mr. Wood.

Here are two possible responses:

THE BUS MONITOR. Mr. Wood is the children's favorite bus driver. My guess is it takes at least five or ten minutes longer to load, and our driveway is so small the other buses can't load. I've spoken with him and he smiles, nods, and says, "What can I do?" I can tell the other bus drivers are pretty impatient with him. He's sort of the senior driver and they don't really speak to him. I say, "Mr. Wood, we get way behind schedule and the parents complain, the other bus drivers complain. Couldn't you just greet them so they keep on moving?" 🌾

MR. WOOD. I just love driving my bus. I know every child and family on my route. They are like family to me. I've been picking them up for ten years now and I give them their first ride to school and when they leave in sixth grade I wave them on. They tell me about their tests and the books they are reading. I know they'd like me to speed up. But how do you speed up a family that wants to tell you all about their sorrows and joys? I just don't know how. 🌾

Writing from a particular point of view requires that you role-play—crawl inside that character, gaze through his or her eyes, and present his or her reactions. See pages 17–21 in *Inside Writing* for more help on how to do this.

1A. You think kids should be coached on the multiple-choice format of standardized reading tests. Write about your reasoning and your coaching methods.

_____
_____
_____
_____
_____
_____
_____
_____
_____
_____
_____
_____
_____
_____
_____
_____
_____
_____
_____
_____
_____
_____
_____
_____
_____
_____
_____
_____
_____
_____
_____
_____

1B. You think standardized reading tests are silly and inaccurate. Write about your reasoning and how you prepare your students for these tests.

2A. It seems many things crowd your day and make it difficult for you to teach. Today, your school is bringing in a historian to speak to the whole student body. Write about how student assemblies can hurt your teaching.

_____
_____
_____
_____
_____
_____
_____
_____
_____
_____
_____
_____
_____
_____
_____
_____
_____
_____
_____
_____
_____
_____
_____
_____
_____
_____
_____
_____

2B. You would be happy to learn something about history and are glad the historian will address the whole student body for the event. This place needs more school spirit, and assemblies are a place to start. Write about how student assemblies help your classroom and school.

3A. On lunchroom duty you notice how much food kids are throwing away. You also notice the snacks kids are eating. It is almost all junk food. Some kids eat only candy and soda for lunch, and it is packed by their parents. You're frustrated because you know all that sugar will cause them to misbehave in your classroom later. Write about this.

3B. You're a working single parent with little time to pack lunches or supervise the lunch your child is packing for himself. You're doing the best you can, but everyone seems eager to criticize. Write from the parent's point of view.

_____

_____

_____

_____

_____

_____

_____

_____

_____

_____

_____

_____

_____

_____

_____

_____

_____

_____

_____

_____

_____

_____

_____

_____

4A. You believe faculty meetings are pointless; nothing is accomplished. Write about that.

4B. You are a school principal and believe faculty meetings are the best way to communicate information to the teachers on your staff. Write from the principal's point of view.

_____

_____

_____

_____

_____

_____

_____

_____

_____

_____

_____

_____

_____

_____

_____

_____

_____

_____

_____

_____

_____

_____

_____

_____

_____

5A. You're upset by the noise coming from the new teacher's room next
door. Write about your concerns or attempts to help.

_____

_____

_____

_____

_____

_____

_____

_____

_____

_____

_____

_____

_____

_____

_____

_____

_____

_____

_____

_____

_____

_____

_____

_____

_____

5B. You're a new teacher with an unruly class. You don't know how to control the students and are worried about your first evaluation and what other teachers are thinking. Write from the new teacher's point of view.

POETRY

If you've never written a poem before, a *list poem* is a great way to start. Here is an example prompt, followed by a sample quick write.

I am the person who . . .

I am the person who starts
The day with coffee, raisin bran, and juice.

I am the person who loves to run
And has been running for forty-one years.

I am the person who turns in sleep
And can tell you what time it is.

I am the person who has been married
For fifty-one years
To a woman I met three
Days before I graduated from college.

Try to end each line with a solid noun or verb.

Try using the concept of a list poem to help you respond to the prompts on the following pages. (For more help in writing poetry, see pages 21–29 in *Inside Writing*.)

1. There were four messages on your answering machine today. Who left them? What did each person want? Try writing a stanza for each message, only rhyming if you want to.

_____

_____

_____

_____

_____

_____

_____

_____

_____

_____

_____

_____

_____

_____

_____

_____

_____

_____

_____

_____

_____

_____

_____

_____

_____

_____

2. Turn a shopping list into poetry. Write what you'll put in your cart this week and how you feel about those items.

3. When I was ten years old [or any age] . . . (Dexter Harding's prose response to this prompt is shown on the next page. On the DVD, watch Dexter turn this passage into a poem in **Rereading a Text:** "Find the Pulse.")

When I was ten years old we lived in a huge old brick dormitory. Three stories tall with a slate roof and ivy growing up the sides. On the vacations the students all went home and Jeff and I had the whole place to ourselves. We couldn't go in the students' rooms, but almost anywhere else was fair game.

Three floors of spiral staircase.

A huge TV room with chair cushions we could toss around and even build into forts.

A basement like a dungeon. Raw, cracked concrete walls covered with graffiti. A maze of doorless rooms and hallways. Bare light bulbs, mostly burned out, a few windows, broken, cobwebbed and dusty.

4. The first time I flew in a plane . . . (or why I have never flown on one). (See Betty Graves' poem on flying a plane in *Inside Writing*, pages 25–27.)

5. Mosquitos, black flies, spiders, snakes. Begin a poem about one or all of them. (See Betty Graves' poem on spiders in *Inside Writing,* pages 27–28.)

6. I can see my mother (or father) with a spoon and mixing bowl. . . .
Write about her using as many details as possible.

_____

_____

_____

_____

_____

_____

_____

_____

_____

_____

_____

_____

_____

_____

_____

_____

_____

_____

_____

_____

_____

_____

_____

_____

_____

_____

7. The miracle of being a father (or mother) swept over me. . . . Write about your own experience becoming a parent, grandparent, or teacher.

8. Write a poem about the items in your mailbox today or on another day
vivid in your memory.

9. Write a poem in response to something you see or hear on the news. (On the next page, read Dexter Harding's two-voice poem in response to a *Time for Kids* report that school officials in Muskogee, Oklahoma, twice suspended Nashala Hearn, 11, because her head scarf, called a hijab, worn as part of her Muslim religious beliefs, violated the school's dress code.)

What Nashala Might Say

Dexter Harding

You don't know me.
Me, dark skinned, with a scarf around my head.
Me, from Allah, from Koran, from hijab . . .

I PLEDGE ALLEGIANCE TO THE FLAG

It would take some time,
But I'd like us to be friends in this—your place
Of kickball, Spongebob, and pizza . . .

OF THE UNITED STATES OF AMERICA

I can tell you are trying
To educate me—and I love it—the music,
The movies, the jokes, and the games . . .

AND TO THE REPUBLIC

Yet, you seem more disgusted
Than interested in my stories of my far-off home:
The food, the dances, the stories . . .

FOR WHICH IT STANDS

And my father says
This country is our greatest hope and chance
To prosper and thrive without fear . . .

ONE NATION,

He says this country was founded
By people willing to die for what they believed:
Freedom, equality, individuality . . .

UNDER GOD,

Your teacher leads this prayer
Please know—I want to *be* part of your free nation,
But not under your god.

WITH LIBERTY AND JUSTICE FOR ALL.

10. Choose a child in your class and write a poem from that child's point of view. (Two poems by Don Graves in response to this prompt appear on the following pages.)

Ms. Burns Won't Let Me Be

Ms. Burns won't let me be.
She's on my case all day long.
She says, Focus on your work.
I try but I can't do it.
Marco wants to talk to me.
Amadeo makes a funny face.
And I get to laughing,
Again she says, Focus.
I hate that word.
I hate doing my papers
With words I don't know.
She says, You'll get behind.
I know I'll never catch up.
Never in a thousand years
Will I ever catch up.

Some days she's nice;
She knows about Sullivan.
I thought she'd yell when
I tripped Amadeo,
But she was quiet
And nice; she's really
Very pretty and I like
The way she smells
First thing in the morning.

One Day

One day, three years ago,
When the fire engines
Were screaming in the streets
And smoke was in the air,
I heard about the terrorists
Who drove planes
Into the twin towers.

I asked Mama
Who did that,
And she said there are people
Who hate us,
Who hate our country.

I asked her
Do they hate me?
No, they don't hate you,
They just hate us
All together.

We talked about it
At school; it was on the radio,
On TV, and I still wonder
What we did
To make them so angry,
That they'd give their lives
Just to punish us.

When I go to bed
I wonder what
I have done wrong
To bring so much hate.

LETTERS INTO ESSAYS

The origin of the essay is the letter. As an example, in five minutes I dashed off the following email to Penny about how testing is driving me crazy.

> Dear Penny,
>
> I was speaking with a friend yesterday who said, "If we could just have one test for the year that would be fine. I know we have to evaluate. What really happens is there is the big state test in the spring and three or four local tests to get ready for it. When do I teach?"
>
> People at so many levels need information on which to base their judgment of a class, school, or system. I ask, "Do they talk to each other? Do they ever chat with teachers to get the sense of what is going on here?"
>
> Testing displaces an enormous amount of teaching time. Testing is not teaching. When a child is taking a reading test, he isn't actually reading something he or she wants to learn. Reading on tests is a totally different genre.
>
> I knew you'd want to know how I think—as if you didn't know already.
>
> Don

Penny writes back, "You should send that to the newspaper." So I go back to the email and make the language more universal. My passion is not diminished; essays are not dispassionate. But they must contain hard facts. Here's my essay.

Have you visited a school lately? Have you actually spoken with a teacher? Ask one simple question, "Tell me about testing for your children. How many do you have? How do you prepare?" Chances are the teacher will report many layers of assessment in reading and mathematics. There are local tests, state tests, and federal tests. There are many people out there who want to know. The tests aren't for the children. Rather, they are for someone far away, out of town.

Ask another question, "How much of your teaching time is displaced by assessment?" It is not unusual for testing to take up to about ten hours a month, or more than two hours a week. Some schools allot even more time, especially schools whose children struggle on tests. Think of all the books the child could be reading during that time. ✺

For more information about turning letters into essays, see pages 29–36 in *Inside Writing*. A number of prompts follow. If you have issues that are closer to your heart, write about them. Write at least two letters or essays.

1. Curriculum has expanded, our time to teach has shrunk, yet assess-
   ments increase daily. If we don't get the time to teach, how can student
   scores improve? *Write a letter or an essay.*

2. Every time I pull up to the pump, the price of gasoline has gone up. How high is it going to get? Who is responsible? *Write a letter or an essay.*

3. Global warming is a major concern. Oceans are rising because of the melting of the ice caps. What's causing this change in our environment? *Write a letter or an essay.*

_____

_____

_____

_____

_____

_____

_____

_____

_____

_____

_____

_____

_____

_____

_____

_____

_____

_____

_____

_____

_____

_____

_____

_____

_____

_____

_____

_____

_____

_____

4. What kind of world will our children inherit? *Write a letter or an essay.*

5. The president and congress talk about our children in passionate tones but it's only lip service; nothing is being done. Children can't vote and their parents don't seem to care the way they used to. Who will stand up for the students in your class? *Write a letter or an essay.*

6. The world has gone nuts over sports and games, and it's created a commercial bonanza. Running a television ad during the Olympics or the Super Bowl costs hundreds of thousands of dollars. We used to enjoy sport for its own sake; now we idolize the big-time athletes and fail to exercise ourselves. *Write a letter or an essay.*

FICTION

Of all the genres, I find fiction the most difficult because I am creating people on paper. What characters say and do must be believable and reveal who they are and what their passions are. Plot follows character. Before you respond to these prompts, turn to pages 36–45 in *Inside Writing,* where the techniques for doing so are discussed in more detail.

Here's a fiction prompt Penny produced for a fifth-grade classroom:

> Quick write an argument between two friends. Be playful; find ways to bring these characters to life. Here's a possible first line if you're stuck: "Gimme the remote." Write for five minutes.

Writing along with her students, this is what Penny wrote.

> "Gimme the remote."
>
> "No. Why?" Sarah didn't want to start another argument with Alexa, so she tried to make her voice less angry than she felt. The problem was—she was angry. Every time Alexa came over she got bossy. How come she always had to be in charge?
>
> "This show is stupid," Alexa challenged. Alexa's voice was quiet, but Sarah knew that was trouble. Alexa was mad.
>
> Sarah sighed and handed her the remote. "Take it."
>
> "Are you sure?" Alexa asked in a sweet voice. It made Sarah want to scream.

"Yes, I don't want it." Sarah could feel tears starting at the back of her eyes.

Sarah's mom came in and said, "What do you girls want to do for dinner?" Sarah thought about pizza: cheesy, stringy, bubbly, spicey—her favorite food ever. But Alexa hated pizza. Sarah felt Alexa jab her in the side.

"McDonald's," Sarah whispered, avoiding her mother's eyes.

Alexa smiled. "I love McDonald's," she said.

Sarah just stared at the darkness out the window and thought, *Alexa has a power over me; what can I say? I'm afraid to make her mad so I just do what she says.* ✺

She then emailed this snippet to me, and I nudged her to reread: *Reread from the standpoint of what the characters want. Make all things in harmony with the want: the appearance, the language, the gestures.*

Penny thought about her characters and decided:

Sarah wants Alexa to be happy—to be her friend. I remember struggling with this when I was about ten or eleven, which is the age I imagine these two to be. I didn't want my friends to be angry and want to go home, but I also let them walk on me sometimes. I want Sarah to stand up for herself—and she wants that, too.

Alexa wants to make all of the choices. Perhaps she doesn't get to make many at her house (older siblings?), but she also doesn't want to push Sarah too far and have her end their friendship.

Here are Penny's notes on her rereading.

- The first sentence sits alone and confuses me: who is talking? I'll need to give readers a little more information. Also, it is a pretty hostile phrase and I'm not sure I wanted the argument to be so hot so soon. I'm wrestling with this: is it too strong? I could ask my daughter; she knows how girls talk to each other. I could also eavesdrop on a few girls at school. Dialogue is important.

- Sarah's first instinct is to answer, "No," but then she says, "Why?" She is struggling with standing up for herself. I think that works.

- Third person is too frustrating. I'm going to rewrite it using *I* for Sarah.

- I think a few physical details in the opening sentences would improve the piece and help the writer see not just hear the scene.

With her next class, who were sixth graders, Penny wrote to the same prompt but switched to different characters.

"Where did you get that pencil, Sam?"

He ignored me.

"Sam," I hissed, "that's my new pencil, isn't it?"

He just kept writing, one line after another, making screechy scratchy noises in his journal.

"You jerk," I said. I wanted to grab it out of his hand but I didn't want Mr. Erickson to see me. I wanted to tell on him. I kind of wanted to hit him. "Give it back," I spit, imagining miniature spit balls bouncing off his cheeks.

He slowly looked at me—eyes like a snake—mean little slits. He ran the pencil across his hand. He put one of his grubby fingers on that cute little pink eraser and the other one down by the point. Then—you won't believe this—he snapped it in half against the edge of his desk. My lovely little pencil splintered in two. Sam just watched my eyes and smiled and handed me half.

I hate him. He's an idiot. ✺

Rereading, Penny had the following reactions.

- I like this one better than the two girls on the couch. There's a spirit in Sam that I want to work with more than Alexa's hostility.

- I think my character is too angry too quickly for these two to be good friends. I am going to rewrite it and tone that down if I can.

- I like the line "I hate him" because kids feel that intensity of feeling so much of the time when they are frustrated.

- "Spit" and "spitballs" are too close together.

- I think these two are about eight, but I'm not sure. I'll have to work that out to keep writing and make it authentic.

- What does Sam want? Why is he bugging his friend?

Now it's your turn. Respond to the following fiction prompts. Then reread and evaluate a couple of them and try a rewrite.

1. Imagine a child in elementary school sitting at his desk jingling things in his pockets. What does he carry in his pockets each day? What is he thinking about? What is happening in the classroom around him? Write about him.

_____

_____

_____

_____

_____

_____

_____

_____

_____

_____

_____

_____

_____

_____

_____

_____

_____

_____

_____

_____

_____

_____

_____

_____

_____

2. Regret can haunt a character. Write a scene in which a character does something she or he later regrets.

3. A family lives in a small house on a quiet street just outside of a busy city. Dad has just lost his job and the family has gathered at dinner to discuss what they will do next. Write the conversation.

4. Animal characters are popular in children's fiction. Remember *The Mouse and the Motorcycle* or *Charlotte's Web?* Pick a favorite creature and bring it to life in its natural setting.

5. Write about a character in a historical period that you enjoy reading and learning about. Include as many period details as you can.

_____
_____
_____
_____
_____
_____
_____
_____
_____
_____
_____
_____
_____
_____
_____
_____
_____
_____
_____
_____
_____
_____
_____

QUICK WRITES
FOR CHILDREN

❧

Students are always fascinated by the stories, photographs, quotations, sketches, and songs that I keep in my writing notebook. They often ask, "What are you writing about?" And I tell them. They want to know where writing begins.

Your students see you reading on most school days. Even when you're not teaching, they might see you huddled over the local newspaper. *They know reading matters in your life.* Your students see you use a calculator when grades are due or your checkbook needs to be balanced. They see you figure out how much food to prepare for parent night or how much money it will cost to go on a field trip. *They know math matters in your life.* Your students also hear you discuss politics with colleagues and worry about the chemicals sprayed on the grass in the local park. *They know that social studies and science have real applications in your life.*

What they've been missing for years is seeing their teachers *write*. They need to see you wrestle with a piece you care about: delete and rethink and add details. They want to hear your wish for a piece you're working on and then celebrate with you when you finally write a draft that shows what you mean. Mostly, they want to understand what prewriting really is and which revision tools are useful. They need to see you craft your writing so they can develop a vision for how to craft their own. You are the only one who can show them. They're counting on you.

The following quick writes are triggers you can use to ensure that you and your students write together, quickly and often. The procedure is simple.

1. Read the prompt to the children.

2. Ask the students, "What does what I've just said make you think of? Write about it. After five or ten minutes I will give the signal to stop. You may not be finished but that's okay, because this prompt is just so you can write what comes into your head. (You may want to complete it later, though.) I will do this quick write right along with you."

You want children to develop the sense that there are lots of options for what to write about. What one child writes can be very different from what someone else writes. But that's the point. A child should invest himself in the topic in a unique way. After the children have done five or six of these quick writes over several weeks, follow this procedure.

1. Read the prompt for the quick write.

2. Ask the students to, "Make a list of two or three things you could write about in relation to what I just said. Then choose one and write."

Don't forget—it's very important that you respond to the prompts along with your students.

I have included a few prompts to get you started, but Penny and I have found that children's poetry or short scenes from children's literature prompt richer responses. I suggest you draw from your favorite authors, short articles from the newspaper, or artwork (as Lucie demonstrates on the DVD in **Choosing a Topic**: "Quick Writes") to inspire quick writes in your classroom.

1. The other day I heard a cat crying in an alley. Well, I think he was crying. He sure was making a loud noise. I don't have a pet and it hit me that maybe I could take the cat home and tell my mom he was lost and had nowhere to go. Have you ever tried to get your parents to buy you a pet? Write about that or any other pet stories you would like to share.

2. Pet owners sometimes argue that dogs can love you but cats couldn't care less about you. Well, when I'm reading my book, my cat jumps up on my lap, nuzzles my neck, and never stops purring. I don't care what people say; cats *can* love you. Write about how you spend time with your favorite animal, in as much detail as possible.

3. Some people don't consider it a sport, but I like to throw rocks. I get a rock about the size of a walnut and throw it at a pile of other rocks I've set up about fifty feet away. I'm getting pretty good at knocking the rocks over. Write about your favorite sport or free-time activity.

4. I'm the third-fastest kid in fifth grade. I'm pretty short and some of the girls have long legs. Two of the girls win every time we have a race. Then they say, "Ha ha, you'll never win." I think I'll go out and practice. Write about the games you play at recess.

_____

_____

_____

_____

_____

_____

_____

_____

_____

_____

_____

_____

_____

_____

_____

_____

_____

_____

_____

_____

_____

_____

5. Someone stole my brand-new bicycle. It was right by the steps in front of my house. I went in to get my backpack and when I came back it was gone. I reported it to the police but I don't think they'll ever find it. They're looking for stolen cars. I know my bike and it has a lock with a chain right under the seat. I borrowed my friend's bike to look for it. What am I going to do? I can't ride with my friends any more. Can you remember a time when you lost something that mattered to you? Write about it.

_____

_____

_____

_____

_____

_____

_____

_____

_____

_____

_____

_____

_____

_____

_____

_____

_____

6. My coach is cool. He sees everything, good and bad. He never bawls us out, but he has a way of making us want to be the best. Know what I mean? My friend and I practice dribbling and shooting. We play hard so that when we get to practice he'll see we've been working on the fundamentals. We want to be the best. Write about the kind of coach you have.

7. I miss my grandma. She's so much fun when she's here, but she lives so far away. She only comes to visit once a year. Write about someone special in your family.

_____

_____

_____

_____

_____

_____

_____

_____

_____

_____

_____

_____

_____

_____

_____

_____

_____

_____

_____

_____

_____

_____

_____

_____

_____

8. My brother and I share the same bedroom. He's older than I am and has his things. But I've got my things too, in a special place. But sometimes I leave a game on my table and my brother walks off with it. He doesn't ask; he just takes it without permission. That really makes me mad. Write about what it is like with your siblings at your house, or write about being an only child. Try to think of just one story and write that story.

9. My Aunt Jill is so neat. She isn't married and takes me down to the mall. We look at all the fashions and jewelry. I watch her try on coats and dresses. She really wants my opinion. Then she takes me to lunch; we have pizza. I feel so special when I'm with my Aunt Jill. Write about a special member of your family or a close family friend. What do you like to do together?

10. I hate to clean my room. Mom says my room is a disaster. Stuff here. Stuff there. My clothes are all over, on the chair, under the bed. But I can find anything when I need to. She says she can't tell what's dirty and what's clean. Write about your room.

_____

_____

_____

_____

_____

_____

_____

_____

_____

_____

_____

_____

_____

_____

_____

_____

_____

_____

_____

_____

_____

_____

11. Our bus is a zoo. We drive the bus driver nuts. He keeps shouting at us to quiet down and says his job is to get us to school and home safely. But how can he do his job when we make so much noise and go up and down the aisles? Write about how you get to school each day.

12. It always happens. About three blocks into the ride I remember I've forgotten my homework. It's in my library book. I didn't really need my library book but I need my homework. I did the homework, I know it well, but I'm getting a check minus in the teacher's book because I forgot it. My mother says I need to learn responsibility. What happens is I'm usually late for the bus and I start grabbing things, lunch money, books. Does this happen to you? Write about what morning is like at your house.

13. I can't stand asparagus. It's like eating grass. When I finish chewing it, I spit out the strings. The smell of it makes me choke. But my mom says, "Just eat one forkful." That's enough to kill me. Write about a food you hate.

14. What's your favorite dessert? Mine is chocolate ice cream. Come to think of it, I like anything chocolate. M&M's are my specialty. My hand keeps reaching into the bag and it can't stop. Write about your favorite dessert.

15. We have big dinners at our house. About twice a year all my cousins come, my gramma, my grampa, my uncles and aunts. There's a lot of noise. Write about a time when your whole family gets together.

_____

_____

_____

_____

_____

_____

_____

_____

_____

_____

_____

_____

_____

_____

_____

_____

_____

_____

_____

_____

_____

_____

_____

_____

_____

16. How do you survive without a best friend? Timmy and I have known each other since first grade. He lives just down the street from me and our parents know each other. We watch the same TV programs and we're Red Sox fans. He likes Manny and I like Ortiz. We even read the same books. Write about your best friend and what you like to do together. (Dexter Harding's response to this prompt is on the next page. You might want to share this with students, or write your own and share that instead. An example will open up the topic in ways students might not have imagined.)

In sixth grade I had a friend named David. But everybody called him Froggy. I don't know why we called him that. It probably started with some silly joke and grew to a nickname. I think he liked it.

At recess we played handball or Frisbee or flipped baseball cards against the wall.

There were groups of kids in that school's sixth grade. Groups of guys that hung together. Groups of girls. My group was Froggy and Mark Harman, Joel Abramson, and Mike Anderson. We sat together in Mr. DeCosta's class, had sleepovers on weekends, and played together most every recess.

One day at recess we were playing hardball and another guy, Mike Gum, stole Froggy's hat and it was our group against his group trying to get it back, but those guys were faster than we were. They were taunting us—"Come on babies, don't you want it back?" And I got this hot feeling in my head and chest—being nervous and angry and afraid all at once and I stuck out my foot as Mike Gunn flew by with Froggy's hat and tripped him. He went crashing to the pavement and everything got silent like in a cowboy movie. 🏃

(Watch Dexter share this quick write with his class in **Rereading a Text:** "Find the Pulse.")

17. I like it when our teacher reads to us. When she reads her voice casts a spell and I'm lost in the book she is reading. So when I pick up that book I can hear her reading from the page. It is like her voice is saying the words. Does that ever happen to you? Write about a favorite book that someone read out loud to you.

_____
_____
_____
_____
_____
_____
_____
_____
_____
_____
_____
_____
_____
_____
_____
_____
_____
_____
_____
_____

FINAL REFLECTION

You have experimented with doing the quick writes. At first you may have struggled to find your voice. But then, after maybe eight or nine quick writes, we hope you began to get rumbles of your voice rising in the text. You said, "That sounds like me." You sensed which quick write selections were best for you.

Of course, the reason for working in the *My Quick Writes* notebook is to help you find your voice but it is also a means to help you write with your children. Teaching in this manner simply saves time. When you put your writing on the overhead you are showing the children why people write. It isn't just an assignment; it is something you want to do. It also shows how writers think and the types of decisions they make.

Go back and choose some of your best quick writes and share them with the children in class. Copy them, make a transparency, put them on the overhead, or chat about how the topic came to you. Children are always fascinated by the lives and thoughts of their teachers.

You will also find help on the *Inside Writing* DVD. You will notice that Dexter Harding, Sue Ann Martin, Vicki Hill, and Lucie Swain use their own writing to teach the children. Of course, all of them began to write alone before bringing their texts to the class. More importantly, they are all involved in small writing groups (three or four other teachers) in their buildings. (See "Teaching Yourself to Share" in the **Conferring** section on the DVD.)

When you write, you feel energy as your voice emerges. Take it one step further and share your writing with the children. Still more energy will emerge. Enjoy the journey!